MW00938929

THE ENEMY INSIDE ME

BRANDI BENSON

The BRAG Media Company
Lagos. New York. London.

The Enemy Inside Me.

Copyright 2018 by Brandi Benson.

All rights reserved. No part of this book may be reproduced, stored in a retrieval system, or transmitted in any form or by any means, electronic, mechanical, photocopying, recording, scanning, or otherwise, without the prior written permission, except in the case of brief quotation embodied in reviews or critical articles. The views expressed in this book are those of the author and are provided for motivational & informational purposes only. While every attempt has been made to provide information that is both accurate, the author does not assume any responsibility for the use/misuse of the information.

Published by The BRAG Media Company

This book may be ordered from booksellers. For bulk purchase contact

brandi@brandilbenson.com

www.BrandiLBenson.com

Printed in the United States

ISBN: 978-1-730981531

DEDICATION

While deployed in Iraq in 2009, I found myself leaving the battlefield early to fight a different kind of fight, one that didn't involve my M16 or our great nation, but my life and a rigorous regiment of chemotherapy: Ewing Sarcoma cancer. This book is dedicated to all the soldiers, those deployed with me and those I never met, who came back with cancer, missing limbs, and scars that we cannot see.

Disclosure*: Some names, dates, and locations have been changed for an individual(s) protection.*

CONTENTS

FOREWORD

The Enemy Inside Me is a *"Super Soul Sunday"* kind of book:

1. It is compact, so you can start and finish it in one Sunday.
2. It's a mind, body, and soul read that you can totally see Oprah dissecting under her giant oak tree.

I appreciate the way the events are ordered in the book and the honesty in the testament. It's a hell of a story with many (real) twists and strains. Though I've never experienced cancer personally or have ever served in the military, I didn't feel left hanging as a reader. Brandi did a wonderful job of explaining concepts—not to the point of boredom but enough for readers to grasp understanding and continue on in the story.

Thought-provoking and well-presented, I was entertained, educated, and empowered. This is a wonderful, inspiring read that I highly recommend to those directly and indirectly affected by cancer and seen/unseen battle wounds.

– **Trelani Michelle** (*Writer, Editor and Teaching Artist*)

INTRODUCTION

The Enemy Inside Me: A Memoir that chronicles my experience being deployed to Diwaniya, Iraq, only to end my tour months earlier than expected, setting down my M16 and picking up the harsh treatments of chemotherapy. Basic training had taught me how to fight, how to use a gun, throw grenades, how to push past my physical limits, combat techniques, and how to defend my country—but this was a different kind of battle. It crept up on me like a stealth enemy in the night. I was not ready for such an attack from within. I was only 24 when I was diagnosed, in a foreign place without the support system of the family I'd left behind. In addition to the very real attack on my body, my soul was also under a kind of attack. I ached for home, for something familiar. I was in the middle of a war and this very thought mounted great fear in my heart. In the midst of these attacks, I almost lost myself.

Through personal journal entries that include timestamps and locations, I revisit the critical moments from that period in my life, from discovering my tumor to being officially diagnosed and preparing my mind and body for treatment. These moments are peppered with emotional flashbacks that expose my fear of death and my thoughts on karma, as well as my struggling marriage and my investigation into the cause of my cancer. It is my hope that this book gives an honest representation of my thoughts and moods during this time, exploring the highs as well as the lows while holding nothing back.

I did not endure this challenging and transforming experience alone. My mother, Tippi Benson, and my nephew, Donavin, supported me in every way possible. At times, their emotional and spiritual support were the only things that lifted me from the clouds of depression and gave me the last push into survival mode. Because of them, I am here today and sharing my story and experience from the battlefield to the hospital room, to the pages of this book.

I remember when I first got to Walter Reed Medical Center, specifically how devastated I was. I wondered if anyone else had the same type of cancer I had. One thing was for sure, I couldn't wait to cry and hear my mother's voice pleading that everything was going to be okay. No one can be ready for cancer; it's an aimless bullet with anyone's name on it.

While I was there, I met some really amazing soldiers. Most were from deployment like I was and in even closer proximity to the burn pit than I. In the first weeks of my arrival, I met a woman named Sweet who offered me sincere and genuine advice while I waited for my first chest x-rays. With her pale skin and sunken honest, brown eyes, she told me that I was strong. I tried to believe her. We chatted for a moment before I was wheeled off, and I cried and hid behind a Kleenex tissue.

I just didn't know what I was in for. I didn't know what to expect. But in those months, I learned that the scariest moments in life are the unfamiliar, the unknown, but there can be no personal growth without discomfort.

My last cycle of treatment was bittersweet. Somehow among the turmoil, I had managed to make some really great memories in room 7130. I made amazing friends with the nurses, doctors, and patients. I had survived a hell of a ride and became a better person. I was weak from all the poison my body had endured, my hair was long gone, and my skin was pale, but my spirit was high.

Before I left the very hospital that saved my life, I was asked by a nurse to speak to a new incoming patient that had just recently been diagnosed with breast cancer and to cheer her up. I did just that.

I walked into Sweet's old room and turned the corner to see a beautiful woman smiling at me. She had a long blonde bob and blue eyes. Tucked under the hospital blanket, she quickly sat up. Her energy was high, her voice was strong, and her eyes held my attention. She reminded me of when I first arrived, eager to hear advice and face the ugly truth of what lay ahead. I sat down toward the foot of the bed and introduced myself.

"I'm Brandi Benson."

And at that very moment it hit me. I did it. I survived. I felt like a hero.

"Amanda Fields... I have breast cancer." She was petrified. I could hear it in her voice, but I never judged her.

She explained to me that she was a schoolteacher. Her students made her a get-well poster, which hung high in the corner of her new room. She stressed her concerns about losing her hair and wondered out loud what her treatments would be like. She was a mother of two younger children and her husband was back home taking care of them. I listened with an open mind and heart, realizing that everyone's story is different, full of different details that get up to the climax. But the motivation is always the same. We want to live and beat the disease of cancer. That's what our stories had in common.

I placed my hand on her knee. "Everything is going to be okay, you hear me?" I said. "Yes, you will lose your hair and look like Mr. Clean for a while." I grazed my baldhead and smiled. "It's extremely cold without hair, so make sure you get a good wig or hat."

Amanda laughed and tugged on her hair.

"But hair grows back," I continued. "I know how you feel. I know the fears you're against. This is going to be the biggest mental game that you have ever played with yourself."

Amanda's eyes swam with tears. "I just don't want to die."

"And you won't," I said, squeezing her knee. "You have to stay positive. You need your family to be a great support system. Watch funny movies and laugh. Listen to your body and rest when you can. Don't see yourself as having cancer. See yourself as being well. And know that your good and happy thoughts are 10 times stronger than the negatives ones."

"Miss Brandi Benson, your mother is at the elevator waiting for you." It was the nurse, Garcia.
I took one last look at Amanda and gave her a hug.

"You're going to be okay. Everything is going to be okay. In a few months, it will be you giving some new patient this pep talk." We both smiled and I walked out of the room and out of that chapter in my life.

If I could offer advice for anyone picking up this book looking for solace, just know the situation that you are in is only temporary. The disease doesn't define you or limit you. This experience had a huge impact on who I am today, of course. In addition to no longer taking my health for granted, I feel stronger and more solid in my beliefs. It made me a survivor.

CHAPTER 1.

LAST GOODBYE

February 10, 2009
0900 hours
Walter Reed Medical Center, Washington, D.C.

I sat on the bed of my small hospital room with my mom while my nephew played in the corner. Walter Reed Medical Center in Washington, D.C. was my new home, and I was the new patient on Ward 71 on the seventh floor. I peered at the fabric of my blanket and began picking at the lint.

Everything is going to be okay, Brandi," my mother said as she fished for more pudding in the small plastic cup she was holding. Another 20 calories met my lips and she forced a smile, showing her crooked teeth. "We have to stay strong and hopeful. You're going to be okay, Brandi." She climbed in the bed with me and I rested my hand on her protruding left rib and embraced her.

The smell of iodoform and harsh bleach stinging my

nose was a constant, and the many doctors and nurses hurrying about only solidified my fears. My mother, Tippi, had up and quit her job after finding out my current condition and moved to Walter Reed, not knowing if she would have a place to sleep or money to buy food. Luckily, the Army, my employer, granted her a place to live and a stipend. My mother would now become my Non-Medical Attendant (NMA) to take care of me.

I was terrified, and it meant the world that my mother was there with me. For my mother, getting up and leaving all that she knew and all that she worked hard for was easy for her. She grew up a military brat for the most part and was used to moving around frequently. As a young girl, her life was full of pain and zero guidance. I'm even more thankful that she was able to stay strong for me in my own time of weakness when I think about what my mother went through in her childhood.

Back then, in 1973, President Nixon suspended all US offensive action in Vietnam, "Angie" by the Rolling Stones boomed on every radio station, a gallon of regular gas was $0.39 cents, and a new military family moved to Maryland. Upstairs in her mother's bedroom, a little girl decided to play dress up. She happily draped a string of pearls around her tiny neck and pranced around in heels too big for her. The pearls swayed from side to side and rested at the bottom of her hand-me-down t-shirt. She walked clumsily over to the edge of her mother's flower-printed bed and hopped up to take a seat. With the pearls gently resting in her lap, both of her tender hands gripped an imaginary steering wheel as her feet swam through the air. "Zoom, zoom, beep, beep."

Checking herself in the mirror in front of her, she smiled. Her reflection showed a five-year-old girl with brown silky straight hair and big brown frog eyes that took up most of her round face. Next to her is the house phone. She picked it up, laughed and giggled then placed it to her ear. "Hello, mommy? Yes, I will pick you up from school," she said and put the phone back down on her side. "Zoom, zoom, beep, bee—"

The bedroom door swung open. "Why are you up here playing?" He rushed over and grabbed the little girl by her hair and threw her to the ground. The little girl glanced up to see a familiar hand hovering over her petrified body. He hurled her into the hallway and beat her unmercifully, delivering a swift kick to her ribs that sent her flying further down the hallway. She crawled, desperately looking for a way out, on her hands and knees as the pearls dragged with agony. He took the princess phone and threw it with such force that it bounced off of her back and clattered out of the hallway. The telephone skidded out to the middle of the wooden floor, spinning on its back, pointing at her mother's bedroom, pointing at the abusive man, pointing at the girl sobbing uncontrollably. One hand cradled her left broken rib, and her free hand was tangled in pearls. The little girl was left in the hallway broken, beaten, and bruised. Her body wept and shook. She faded to black before passing out from the pain. This little girl is my mother.

The same little girl is now cheering me on in a hospital room as black mascara tears traced down my face and collected at the base of my chin only to drop onto my white hospital gown as snot dribbled down my top lip.

"This just can't be right, Mom," I said. "It can't. This wasn't supposed to happen to me. I don't want to die." More tears and snot fell onto my gown, creating large wet spots that looked like ink stains.

"Everything is going to be okay, Brandi," she repeated, shushing me.

The wrinkles around her face squeezed together as she blotted her eyes. She cast a glance to the corner of the room where my nephew, Donavin, was playing. He was only two years old and could barely talk. Gnawing on soggy graham crackers, he lifted up his other hand that wasn't holding the gummy slop and began exploring the little holes he saw inside the vents by the window. In a stiff and almost mummy like walk, Donavin waddled over. One step. Two steps. Three steps.

"Donavin, stop touching that!" she snapped. "You're going to get hurt!"

My mother was watching Donavin while his mother, my sister, was deployed in Iraq. My mother was an amazing mom. You could never find a more loving and more loyal mother than my mom was. She turned back to me. Her ponytail swept across shoulders and rested at the nape of her golden neck.

"Michelle will be here for her R&R, and she can take him to the playground more," she said, wiping her nose as Donavin stared out the gigantic windows, plopped to the ground, and cried.

My sister, Michelle, was two years younger than me. We were complete opposites. Michelle jammed out to hard-core rock music, while I listened to oldies and preferred R&B tunes. Michelle had a quick tongue, and I was always afraid of hurting people's feelings. At the dinner table, she would throw back her seafood and didn't mind the tentacles on the octopus, while I sat at the opposite end of the table strategically trying to pluck out the veins in the chicken. Scrapping the skin off the chicken breast, I would have a little mountain of discarded flesh on my plate.

"I'm sure he just needs to play outside and not be stuck with us in this room." She looked at the four walls and then down at the empty pudding container. She sighed again.

"But everything is going to be okay. I promise, Brandi. You're a strong girl. This isn't the end for you." I tried to be positive. I wasn't sure how I was going to get through this or how I would adapt to the many changes around me. This new place, this new life, was completely different. I had cancer. It was bad. I knew these facts, had even forced myself to say them out loud in the mirror as an effort to come to terms with my new situation. But I was determined to not let this disease inside me paralyze me. I had to be hopeful for the future and not get lost in the clouds of my depression.

I tightened the bandana on my head as clumps of hair fell on my pillow. All positivity left me and my body folded over with deep guttering sobs.

"I'm so scared, Mom," I said, trying to speak through my tears. She rubbed my back and shushed me, but she was crying too now. As I sat there, crying and rocking back and forth, I couldn't help but think back to my grandfather's last day.

July 11, 2004
1100 hours
North Shore, Hawaii

When I was 20 years old, I watched my grandfather pass away from lymph node cancer. The hospital had recently released him, so he spent his last day overlooking the beautiful waters of the North Shore in Hawaii on my aunt's patio. The rain was coming. I remember the earthy smells of the tropical ferns and the blur of blackbirds that dove from the branches of the surrounding trees to the underbrush below, where they landed effortlessly with the dried up plumerias and the fallen leaves. The rattling branches shook, lightning forked in the air and a loud roar of thunder rolled across the Hawaiian land. And in the middle of all that beauty, all that nature, my grandfather sat on the patio—too weak to hold his head up.

His mouth hung open like his jaw muscles couldn't

find the strength to keep it closed. I was struck by how skinny he was, how much his bones protruded from his skin, now the texture of old leather. This was not my grandfather. Six short months ago, this man was full of life, laughter, opinions, love, and advice. But before us now was a lifeless puppet ready for the show to end. It was a painful death, to say the least, and I had a front-row seat.

We were all there—his wife, his children, and his grandkids. We sat by his side, taking turns saying our goodbyes and getting one last look at this once-vibrant man. When it was my turn to say farewell, I recall looking into his lifeless eyes and staring down into his dry mouth. Those eyes cast an emptiness that I had never seen before, a sort of pathetic and tired apathy. My grandfather knew what was coming. His eyes told me that he could feel he wouldn't be here too much longer and he'd given up.

I was looking at death in the face; even the bravest of souls would be petrified. My skin prickled as I nervously wet my lips and sat next to him. I traced my hand on his arm and ran my fingers down until I met his tense hands. His arms used to bear strength from all the years as a police officer, but now they looked weak, arranged at his sides as if he was already in a coffin. Again, I found myself trying to compare the man I had made memories with to the man there with a lifeless expression resting on his face. That man from before was gone and I had to accept that.

I placed my hands on his and thanked him for being

there for me. I thanked him for bailing me out of trouble a few years back when I had gotten arrested for drinking underage. If it weren't for him, I would have missed my high school graduation and spent the weekend in a county jail. One simple call from him got me out.

As we sat together, I told him not to be afraid. I closed my eyes and listened to the palm trees as the wind blew softly through my hair. The humid air twisted in my nostrils as the ocean waves crashed against the rocks and burped up seaweed. I opened my eyes once again, and leaned over and whispered in his ear:

"You did a great job here. You're a strong fighter, but it's time to go home. You will be happy. No more pain, grandpa. No more pain."

Unclasping my fingers from his, I blew him a last kiss goodbye. A gust of wind raced through space between us, causing the sand on the patio outside to shuffle. My dark brown strands of hair whirled wildly as they touched the bridge of my nose.

Walking away from my grandfather that morning was hard, but I knew he was going to a better place—a blissful place where his soul could run free again.

I reunited with the rest of my family in the house and we all watched from the window as his health deteriorated. My grandfather had warred against a fierce enemy and lost. Chemotherapy couldn't even help. Seeing how much it changed him, how much of his spirit was gone, I knew from then on I didn't want to be a sorrowful victim of the devil's game. Then again, who really plans on battling with this cruel disease? In the end, the blanket of death will cover us all no matter how we live our lives. Death is an enemy we will never escape.

I didn't know it then, but I was soon going to be facing the same beast that stole my grandfather away. Soon, doxorubicin would be screaming through my veins like an ambulance on the highway, depleting all of my energy. I'd be weak and crying in a hospital gown, unable to lift my head up. Would people look at me in pity the same way we watched my grandfather on his last day, remembering the things I was once good at, the girl I once was? Or would I become a memory told from the lips of my mother?

February 10, 2009
0905 hours
Walter Reed Medical Center, Washington, D.C.

Snapping back to reality, I gripped my hospital blanket 'til my knuckles turned white, and I saw my mother had moved from the bed and was now coddling my crying nephew. I never thought I would have cancer. I never saw this coming. At the age of 24, I was preparing myself for other things. I didn't go to school on how to beat terminal illnesses. I imagined my life much different. A year ago, I played on a college soccer team, surfed and partied with NFL players. I studied for exams, took trips back to the mainland, and hiked steep mountains. I fixed my hair and did my makeup. I was a normal 24-year-old. But now, a hostage in my own body, I kept wondering how this had happened to me and how I could've possibly missed all the signs.

CHAPTER 2.

HOMESICK

March 4, 2008
1300 hours
Army Recruiting Office Gurnee, Illinois

Inside my recruiter's office, I took the chance to look around a bit. Piles of paper were stacked high everywhere—contracts, memos, printed out emails, letters of awards, job descriptions. Directly behind him sat a thick frame with the Soldier's Creed inside. "I just need you to sign here."

My Army recruiter pointed to a spot on the paper. "Hey, does your mother still not know that you're joining?" he asked.

"That's right," I said, looking up at him. "And I would appreciate it if you didn't say anything to her."

He shrugged like he saw this all the time. "It's just...she thinks it's too dangerous."

My mother didn't approve of the idea of both of her daughters in the Army. Her worst nightmare was that we'd both get deployed at the same time and that something horrible would happen.

"Sign here and here and here," he continued, pointing at the paper, smacking his lips together as he spoke. "You'll be all ready to head out next month. Make sure you stay in the gym now. Basic ain't no joke. You don't want to be a fat slob like me."

"Thanks," I replied cheerfully. "I will. And the Army will pay off all my student debt, pay for me to go to college, and I can try out for the All-Army teams, right?"

"That's right," he said, gathering the papers I signed and stapled them.

I knew my mother was worried, but I was sold. How could I pass up a golden opportunity like this? Free schooling, no debt, and a jump-start in a career. I wondered why others didn't do the same. My first day in the Army would be April 4, 2008, and boy was I in for a culture shock.

April 4, 2008
1900 hours Basic Training
Fort Jackson, South Carolina

I had finally made it to basic training at Fort Jackson in South Carolina. The entire day and evening, we spent hours going through all the new soldiers' bags, waiting in line, repeating our social security numbers, and breaking up into the groups we would stay with until graduation. After the tedious inspection, we were able to get some rest. Or that's what I thought at least.

0300 hours

"Wake up!"

I heard boots slapping the floor and a crisp uniform trucking by. The noise reminded me of the sound my nylons would make when I crossed my legs in church. I looked up and a solid woman wearing a camouflage uniform stomped past me. She was thick with thighs like ham hocks and feet that shook the ground.

"Time to get up, up, up, you lazy bitches." She flicked the light switch on. "Welcome to the real world. Now get the fuck up!" She had sharp features like a rat—beady eyes, buck teeth, and a thin pencil nose.

I was startled. If this was the real world, I didn't want any part of it. It was only my first day at Fort Jackson in South Carolina and I had barely slept the night before. My sister failed to tell me they treated you like shit in basic training, woke you up in a very rude manner, and verbally assaulted you on a daily basis.

The woman walked up and down, casting glares that could bend steel. "You have 30 minutes to get ready. None of y'all betta not be late!"

As soon as she walked out the door, we all scrambled out of bed. Some went straight to the bathrooms to wash their mouths, others pulled out a brush and a hand mirror, some went back in their beds, and others roamed around aimlessly. I stood in my same spot, frozen and regretting this decision I had made. I wanted to go home, but I was committed for three years.

April 8, 2008
0800 hours Basic Training
Fort Jackson, South Carolina

I had been waiting in the chow line for breakfast for what seemed like years now. The food in basic was okay, but I was craving a number one from Wendy's. All I kept thinking about was the gigantic burger on the commercials rotating slowly, meat so hot it spat up bubbles and leaked with grease. I craved those thick slices of cheese, molding and hugging the beef patty.

"Next group!" barked a drill sergeant. It was finally time to get this dog food.

"Benson, what are you getting today?" It was my battle buddy, Gomez. We had become pretty close over the last few days and shared bunks in basic.

"I'm not sure," I said, turning around to look at her. "Probably some grits and a bagel." She smiled and her sausage lips took up most of her mocha-colored face.

"I'm going to have the same," she said. "But with a lot more shit. Getting a little bit of food would be a big mistake. I don't want to starve again."

Like everything else about the military, there were strict rules concerning when and where we were allowed to eat. Once we got our food from the line, we had five minutes to wolf down our meals. When the drill sergeant said to stop, you had to stop, get up, and take your food to the trash. Sneaking any leftovers into your pockets was not allowed, nor were we allowed to have food or drinks inside our rooms. Getting caught with food or drinks would result in some kind of trouble, so most of us ate as much as we could stomach in each sitting and especially at dinner, knowing it'd be hard trying to sleep on an empty stomach.

"I heard the food is worse in Iraq," I told Gomez as we stood in line. "And we have to ask our families to send us the stuff we want. I heard that the little grocery stores on the Fobs (forward operating base) run out of stuff fast, too. Stuff like face wash and toothpaste."

"I don't use a face wash," she said, and her face testified to years of neglected skin care.

She forged on.

"And Iraq?" she smirked. "Girl, we're not going to Iraq. We're brand new to this shit.

Why would they send us to Iraq?" She winked at me while she kept her tone nonchalant.

"We haven't even broken into our uniforms," she said, her voice rolling over into a playful laugh as she lifted up an arm that was swimming in her baggy uniform.

"Of course, they're gonna send us to Iraq," I said, looking at her like she was stupid. "I mean I hope they don't, but I keep hearing that it's not uncommon for new soldiers to become deployed, right drill sergeant?" I said, now facing the drill sergeant who was standing in front of us in the line. I coated my voice with curiosity.

The drill sergeant whipped his head around and smiled at us with coffee stained teeth.

"Oh, you guys are going to the theater," he said with his eyebrows arched as if he was demanding we go right then. "Don't you worry about that, and I'll most likely read about your deaths in the Army Times. You, new soldiers, need to pay attention." He paused. "I've been deployed eight times and I have made it back every time, but I can't say that for some of my battle buddies."

Gomez and I stood there awkwardly and didn't reply. The drill sergeant moved his beady, caviar eyes to the back of the line.

"Some of you are going to be sliced to bloody ribbons, some of you will come back with no limbs, and some of you will come back with scars that you can't see."

"Next group!" A different drill sergeant was screaming at us to keep the line moving. "Keep it moving, Benson! Don't tie the lineup."

People here were always doing one of two things: yelling or telling me I was going to die soon. Somewhere in between the clanks of the silverware scraping on plastic trays and plastic trays sliding on metal rails, there was another loud voice by the trashcans.

"Time's up! Move it, move it, move it. Don't you dare take another bite, you!"

Months later, I found out that Gomez was wrong. Right after basic and after completing my Advanced Individual Training, the training that pertains to your job in the Army, I was deployed. I was at my first duty station at Fort Carson in Colorado for one month and nine days, and then I was shipped off to Iraq and told that it was my turn to fight for my country—a fight that I wasn't sure I'd been trained for.

CHAPTER 3.

UNEASY FEELING

January 10, 2009
1700 hours Fob Echo
Al Diwaniyah, Iraq

Today, I decided to increase all my reps and weights at the gym. I had been in Iraq for about three months and had a pretty good routine for the gym at Fob Echo. Instead of doing 300 crunches, I would do 500. Instead of running one mile, I was going to run two. I increased all my weights by 10 pounds and only took one-minute breaks in between. I was determined to get a 300 on my Physical Training (PT) test.

After that treacherous session at the gym, I walked back to my containerized housing unit (CHU), climate-controlled trailers where we slept, with the sun beating down hard.

I was tired, but I felt good. I had finally started to dedicate all my free time to the gym, much like all the other soldiers. It was a popular way to pass the time on deployment. There was really nothing else to do besides sleep, eat, and go to the gym. Why not train extra hard and push my body to the limit? My PT Test was scheduled for the following month and I had placed a bet with Private Romero that I could score higher than he could. I wanted to prove to all the other soldiers that females were PT studs too. I planned to score nothing lower than 300, the maximum score that could be achieved in the Army. I had been training since the end of November and I felt like I was ready for this challenge, more physically fit than I'd felt all of my life. Iraq, with the smoke, heat, and dirt, always felt polluted. Walking from the gym to my CHU, I watched the smoke coil mysteriously out of the roof of the dining facility, as it blackened and tangled around the T-walls (20-feet high concrete walls that deflect incoming rounds) that supported the eroded and bent-shaped buildings. The thick black smoke slowly lightened up and disappeared. The gravel gave away as it crunched beneath my feet and a light mist of dust floated about as usual.

Pushing the door open to my little hut, I took a step onto the eroded blackened wood and swiped my shoes across the grass. A slight pain rode up my outer thigh, and I took in a short sharp breath. I was so sore. Even the slightest movement reminded me of my intense training sessions from all week.

"I just need to stretch a bit and lay down," I said to myself. Before I could even manage to ease the door ajar, my roommate welcomed me with a huge smile and swung the door effortlessly wide open.

"How was the workout? You've been gone for a while now." She retreated back to her pallet as her wide hips and beefy thighs rubbed together.

"I was going to wait for you to get something to eat, but you took too long," she said. "Here, I brought this back for you. They only had one left." Flying in the air was a banana nut muffin. My hands quickly grasped the flying food.

"Thanks." Making my way to my bed, I slowly began to kneel down. My muscles were weary and I felt as stiff as solid oak. Nestling my back against my short bed frame, I tilted my head back and gazed at the ceiling. In the top left corner, I noted that rainwater had been leaking through the ceiling, causing ugly black stains that even the strongest of chemicals couldn't wipe away.

"Aaahh, my workout was great," I said to my roommate. "Did legs today. You should have come with me." I served my roommate a mischievous smile. "Do you think you're going to pass the PT test next month?"

There was a slightly awkward pause. My roommate hated the gym and had been avoiding going with me ever since I first met her.

"Hey," I tried again. "Do you think you're going to pass? I can help you. I promise, if you go with me every day to the gym until next month, you will pass!"

I threw my legs out like a rag doll and stretched, casting another glance at my desperate roommate. We both nodded in agreement.

"Okay, I'll go with you to the gym," she replied miserably and tossed her thick locks to the side showing her fleshy neck. "I'll go, but you have to take it easy on me."

"Good!"

Squaring my shoulders, I dropped my head toward my knees and began to push down with my hand. I noticed a peach-sized sphere in my inner left thigh close to my groin area. I showed my roommate.

"Oh my god! What the hell is that?" She seemed more concerned than I was. "That's not normal, Benson." She moved to the edge of her bed. "Is that from working out? If it is, I don't want to go with you anymore. What the hell is that?"

I continued to push it and poke it. "It doesn't hurt or anything," I told her. "I don't know what it is. It will probably go away." I gathered my brittle body and headed down to the showers to get a better look at the lump.

Stepping outside, the smell of burning trash alerted me that it was finally nightfall. I coughed, muffling my mouth with my tired shoulder and tried to keep my noises down for the other soldiers who were trying to get some rest. Off in the distance, I could see the scarlet sparks dashing across the open sky, and I could hear the gentle hissing of the flames as the fire grew and devoured the trash. The bright red and orange colors clashed against the blanketed night for endless hours, leaving a magical burgundy glow.

"What on Earth are they burning?" I thought.

They were supposedly burning trash, but what kind of trash? I imagined the inside of the pit, where flames licked at plastic containers and consumed the old squares of aluminum foil once wrapped around the turkey sandwiches. Or were they burning more substantial materials, like copper or brass? It was rumored they were also burning human feces, but that couldn't be true. Mostly I wondered why they were burning it at all, instead of digging a deep hole and covering it up. I never came face-to-face with a burning pit, but I could only imagine the poor soldiers developing a smoker's cough, and that rattling cough leading to stage four lung cancer.

Back in high school, I remembered being taught about the dangers of rat urine and feces. I learned that it caused viruses like Rickettsia, which creates a condition similar to chicken pox. Hantavirus was another. Eosinophilic Meningitis, caused by rat lungworm, is an infection of the brain. Rat feces, if not disposed of the proper way, is bad for your health.

But no precautions were made with the burn pit, and the soldiers operating the pits didn't see this as a problem. Curtains of black smoke sat thick in the sky, and I tried to imagine huffing toxic fumes for endless hours—throat burning, eyes watering, and a never-ending itch on your skin. The smell of poison was so strong that it made the nearby air go wavy. The thoughts made my stomach turn. Here I was just a few miles away from the burning pits, and I was nagging about the smell of tar and the soot.

I later learned they burned trash when the sanitary and waste management facilities are backed up or not available, but the waste still had to be taken care of. This was considered an "ethical" way to prevent health problems. As backward as this seems, this was still allowed.

January 16, 2009
1700 hours Fob Echo
Al Diwaniyah, Iraq

I was keeping an eye on the lump in my leg, but nothing had changed. I still wasn't experiencing any pain in the area. I only felt exhausted, which I attributed to how much time I'd spent in the gym. I felt a nagging suspicion that I may have just pulled my groin muscle, but wouldn't that hurt?

I even went as far as asking other soldiers what they thought it might be, like my workout buddy, Eddie. Eddie was a tall Mexican guy from Boston who lived and breathed the gym. He was the perfect workout partner and at our next workout session, I decided to ask him what he thought it was.

"Eddie, remember the other day when we did legs?" I asked while he held my feet as I did a sit up.

"Yeah, why?" he replied over the clanking weights and grunts from the far corners of the room.

"Have you noticed anything different in your legs or anything?" He looked at me with eyes as bored as a small deserted island. A treadmill next to us sped up and soldiers shuffled by in front of us.

"Benson, we just did legs the other day. How can I notice anything different? It's not enough time for the muscles to grow," he said sarcastically.

"No, like do you have any bumps or knots in your legs?" I sat up. "Wha?"

"I'll show you." I pulled my PT shorts tight around the bump and we both started laughing.

"Yo, what is that, Benson? That's not normal," he said standing up. He took a step back, squinted his eyes at my leg and started shaking his head back and forth. "When did that happen? Better yet, how did that happen?"

"I don't know," I said, shrugging my shoulders. "The strange thing is that it doesn't even hurt. I guess I should go see Captain May."

CHAPTER 4.

SHIPPING OUT FOR THE BIG SECRET

January 17, 2009
0500 hours Fob Echo
Al Diwaniyah, Iraq

Ugh, why am I so tired? I slowly opened my eyes, lifted the covers off of my warm body and immediately regretted the move. I didn't want to leave my CHU. It was so cold outside. The winters in Iraq were so much different than the ones in Hawaii. Winters in the Middle East were wet and cold, but in Hawaii, it was sunshine and surfing weather. It was a hard adjustment. For now, my uniform and layers would have to do. As I dressed, I felt my body resisting the effort to wake up. I felt dazed and heavy like I had run 15 miles the day before. Sure I was always tired, but this was different. I slung my black M16 over my left shoulder and walked to the dining facility.

Outside, only a few brave stars were left behind, winking periodically. With my teeth chattering, I put my cold hands inside my pockets and proceeded for duty. I yawned uncontrollably the entire walk and the exhaustion sunk deeper and deeper into my bones. My eyes began to sag. The rocks and sand shifted under my Army boots as the icy winds brushed my face and dashed behind my neck, settling into my thin sweater. Every inch of my body wanted to turn around and go back to sleep. My room was blissfully warm and the smells of lavender wafted beautifully inside. My roommate had hung Christmas lights months ago but still hadn't taken them down. I wasn't complaining though, there was something soothing about the way the dull lights created the perfect dimness in our room. It made me feel safe.

It was so quiet during this time of day. It made me feel very uneasy. I could hear the branches rubbing against each other and the distant chants from the Muslims made me check for my weapon's magazine clip. The fluorescent light shone into my eyes and the smells of spices and batter lured me into the dining facility where I was scheduled for extra duty. Still, not even the smell of breakfast could snap me out of my sleepy zone. I needed a few more hours of rest.

Dragging my tired self into the dining facility, I sat down next to Private Roe.

Roe was a bit on the heavy side, with thinning jet-black hair and vigilant eyes that sat oddly apart, but didn't stop him from seeing anything.

"Morning," I said, nodding my head and leaning back in my chair.

"Whooooooa, Benson," he said with a playful smile.

"You look tired, girl! What in the world did you do last night?" His eyes scanned me as he sipped on his black coffee, and tapped his anxious, pudgy fingers on the plastic table.

"No, seriously," he said when I didn't answer. "Why do you look so tired? I didn't want to say anything, but for the last couple of weeks, you have been looking different. Something is different about you!" He reached out his stocky hand and placed it on top of mine.

I yawned and said, "I'm just tired."

"Hey, maybe you should take a break from the gym," he continued. "This bet isn't that serious, Benson. At least, not if you're going to come into work every day looking like death!" His lips curled up and he beamed a goofy smile at me. I could hear the amusement in his mocking voice.

"Shut up, Roe," I finally responded after finding the energy to match his playful tone. "I'm fine! Just tired, that's all. We got 15 minutes before we open. What are you having for breakfast? The same thing? Why don't you mix it up a bit, huh? You're never going to win this bet if you can't eat healthily."

I leaned into him and tapped him on the cheek.

"Come on chump, let's eat," I said pushing myself away from the table. "And don't worry about me. Just worry about me whooping that butt next month." We laughed and headed to the grill for some eggs.

Months ago this dining facility was a bullseye. Flying mortars shells and shrapnel had come crashing down with tremendous speeds, destroying the vicinity—broken cinder blocks everywhere, gaping holes in and out of the area—just completely demolishing this place. Now pictures of the devastation were glued to the walls like souvenirs. Still, under repair, the cold of winter seeped through the cracks of the walls, reminding us of the terror that could strike at any given moment.

0900 hours
After my first shift of duty at the dining facility (DFAC), I went to the medic station, planning to get some answers about the lump in my leg. I walked across the gravel to the sagging building about 50 yards away. The medic center, surrounded by tan sandbags used as shields, looked lifeless. The building was made of cinder blocks with cracked windows and the doors were splintered across from the top and bottom. There was no doorknob present, just a bare hole. One boot in front of the other, I entered the medic station with no hesitation, thinking I was ready for some answers.

This was my first deployment and the first time I was away from my family. I knew they were just a phone call away, but something about this lump was making me uneasy. I still played with the idea that I had simply pulled a muscle, even though I still wasn't feeling any pain. I had pulled several muscles in my leg in the past, but nothing like this had just ever popped up. It didn't hurt me, not even when I touched it, which I often did. It was beginning to feel like something foreign was forming in my body. As I walked into that hospital, I was scared out of my mind. What news was Captain May, my unit's doctor, going to deliver to me? The week before, I had seen her for an abscessed tooth and she took care of that problem right away. Would it be as quick this time?

Familiar faces surfaced through the aid station. A few male officers whispered amongst themselves as they laid eyes on me and began to offer lustful smiles in my direction. While deployed—known as being in the theater—sometimes the lines of fraternization become a blur. There were quite a few rumors about a married E6 and a Captain getting too friendly with each other. I was sure to stay far away from any officers.

"Excuse me," I said to the officer by a table. "I need to see Captain May." I instantly felt heat rise up my bare neck and my cheeks began to color. I could see the curiosity on the officers' faces. I was a little nervous and my palms began to sweat; I hated talking to officers.

"Okay, Benson," he replied with a happy smile. "I'll let her know that you're here to see her. Have a seat real quick over there." He pointed to a corner where there was a folding chair.

"Yes, sir."

Passing by the officers, I observed the sheer feeble beam of light that had managed to pierce through the windowpane, giving off a dismal scarlet glow. The floor cracked in agony. A spider scurried past. I sat down hesitantly and wrapped my boots around the legs of the chairs, moving the cobwebs that weakly detained the legs. With my arms folded across my chest, I moved my head in the direction of the snickering again. The officers continued to laugh and exchange jokes with one another. Every once in a while, they would look back at me. I smiled back with the best of my manners and dropped my head.

A few minutes later, the officer yelled and spat into a water bottle that was full of brown guck and cigarette butts. "Captain May, you have a soldier." His request echoed and bounced off the sheer walls. A petite lady with blonde hair peeked from the corner. "Okay, send her in, please," she said. I was escorted to the same private area as before when I saw her last week for my tooth. With her hand on the middle of my back, she led me to a small stretcher.

"Hey Benson, how did that medication work for you last week? Is your mouth feeling any better?" Her deep blue eyes showed great concern, while she ran her index finger lightly around the rim of a cup of coffee she held in her hand.

"Yes ma'am, my mouth feels a lot better. Thanks. I have another problem, though. But I'm not too sure what it is. Maybe you can help me?"

"Sure," she replied cheerfully. "What's the problem now?" She shifted a chair with her free hand and held the coffee cup in the other.

"Well I have a small bump in my leg," I told her. "But it doesn't hurt and it won't move.

I think I pulled a muscle, but I just want to get it checked out." I placed my hand on my groin area and pulled my pants down tight around it, baring the silhouette.

"Okay, can you please drop your trousers? I need to get a better look at it." Her eyebrows were knitted in confusion. Taking a big gulp of her coffee and placing it to the side, she positioned both of her hands on her knees.

"Sure," I said.

Scrunching the top folds of my jacket, I bit down with my bottom lip and unzipped my top to be a bit more comfortable. Twisting carefully and cautiously, I sucked in my stomach a bit, unfastened my belt, and dropped my pants. I leaned back on the stretcher and lifted my left knee to show her the protruding bump on my leg. Captain May pulled up a chair and got closer to me. A few seconds of awkward silence passed; she seemed dumbfounded. I caught a quick gaze of pity as her confusion surrendered to a conviction. Did she know something? Did she know what this was? Rubbing a spot in between her eyes, she rolled back and stood up.

Oh no, I pondered to myself. It must be a pretty bad strain, why else would she look like she was solving a math problem in her head?

"Mmmm. And you're not experiencing any pain?" She drummed her hand on her chin. Drawing back and interlacing her fingers, Captain May looked as if I had thrown cold water in her face. She excused herself and left the room to get a second opinion about this mysterious lump in my leg.

"I will be right back," Captain May said, as she walked out of the room. "I want Captain Johnson to take a look at this, okay?"

I nodded my head yes and didn't give the idea another thought.

When Captain May and Captain Johnson came back into the room, it was clear that Captain May had caught her up on my story and why I was there in the office. Captain Johnson eyes swept the table I was sitting on and settled on my left leg. Captain Johnson was a chunky Asian lady who looked as soft as homemade fudge in her sweaty PT uniform. It was evident that Captain Johnson was also training hard for the PT test coming up next month.

Small pools of sweat beaded along her hairline and ran down her temple slowly like an iced latte sitting outside on a hot summer day and her arms pits were dark with wet stains.

"Good morning, Benson," she said, wiping her hands on her shorts. "Captain May told me that you found a lump in your leg about a week ago." She rubbed and knotted her fingers together as if she were trying to warm them up.

I shook my head up and down once again.

"Do you mind if I touch it?" Captain Johnson asked.

"No," I said.

Outside, I could hear the soldiers marching back to their offices from the dining facility. Breakfast was now over, and it was time for my first workout for the day. I had already prepared an excuse for why I couldn't do legs today, and I was sure that Eddie wouldn't mind. This lump in my leg was the reason.

Captain Johnson placed her hand around the bump in my leg. She cupped it, poked it, and pushed it.

"Benson was just telling me that it doesn't hurt. Right, Benson?" Captain May added before taking a sip of her coffee.

"Yeah, it doesn't hurt," I said. "Like right now, you're poking it and it doesn't feel like anything."

Captain Johnson's eyes tested me, measuring my response, and she pushed down harder.

"Does that feel like anything? Do you feel pain?" Captain Johnson asked as she squinted her almond-shaped eyes at me.
"Not at all," I replied.

Both Captain May and Captain Johnson exchanged looks among themselves, nodded their heads, and left the office for the second time.

Sitting at the edge of the stretcher, I began swinging my legs and daydreaming about my family back home and my sister who was also in Iraq. Man, it had only been a few months and I was already homesick. All I kept thinking about was that damn PT test next month, calling my family back in the states, and the countdown until I got back home. I couldn't wait to see my mother.

When they returned, they asked a few more questions and ended my visit with the orders to be on the next helicopter to Baghdad in just a few hours. I was told to gather my sleeping gear, my bulletproof vest, and a few uniforms before heading off. I nodded and asked zero questions—partly because they didn't seem concerned and partly because I was learning not to ask questions here. I thought they were just as clueless as I was. The thought of the lump being something detrimental to my health never crossed my mind. I was more than naïve; I was oblivious to all the clues then.

While walking out of the room, I glanced shyly back at the husky officers once again who stood in attendance near the door. I could feel their eyes burning right through me. My cheeks flushed more as I zipped up my top a bit higher and adjusted my uniform. This was the beginning of the end. I was being transferred to Baghdad so the doctors could get a more in-depth look at my leg and run a CT scan. I was more than happy to go. This meant a few days of sleeping in, no work, more time to train, and a chance to see the heart of Iraq.

Tapping the front of my teeth, I kept thinking about how amazing the trip was going to be. Maybe I would see something like in Aladdin, with poor young kids roaming the little markets on the streets, selling trinkets and treasures. I had imagined the children wearing old, ripped-up pants and outdated cartoon shirts, shoes with holes in them, and their skin extremely tan from the blazing heat waves. I saw them stealing to survive, taking from the rich and feeding the poor, emulating Robin Hood. My mind was in a frenzy about my new layover. I was excited. I had my camera phone ready. But I didn't imagine how intense the ride to Baghdad was going to be.

As I walked back to my CHU, the wind tore at the back of my trousers, tossing my patrol cap to the ground where it landed on the gravel ahead of me in a pile of spent shell cases and trash.

Why is it so windy? I thought as I hunched over in the cold and grabbed my cap. Oh, yeah. It's winter, I reminded myself.

I hoped that the weather in Baghdad would be better. Kicking a piece of mortar into the same pile of cigarette butts and empty shell cases, I reminded myself to bring my laptop and earplugs. Lord only knew how bored I would probably get, I thought.

I heard more sounds of marching soldiers in the distance. Catching a glance of the movement ahead reminded me that it was lunchtime. I heard a faint voice saying my name.

"Benson! Hey, Benson!" It was my roommate running towards me.

"Hey." She bent over to catch her breath and pushed her M16 to her side. Her chubby hands rested anxiously on her knees. "I heard you're on the next flight to Baghdad." She suddenly gasped for more air. "How did you pull that off?"

"Yeah," I replied. "Did Captain May tell you I was leaving?"

"Yes, I had to update the manifest for tonight at 2000 hours. Why are you going?"

"I found a lump in my leg a week ago, remember? Just getting it checked out," I replied.

"I'll be fine. If something were wrong Captain May and Captain Johnson would have said something to me. I just need a CT scan that's all. No biggie! I'll be back. I think I pulled a muscle. Been working out too hard, I guess."

"Have a safe flight, Benson. Are you nervous about going in a chopper? I would be if I were you. Did you ever hear about that flight that was shot out of the air?" And she grabbed the butt of her weapon, "Everyone died."

"No," I replied dryly.

1845 hours

Hours had passed and the weak sunrays hid behind a few evening clouds as I sat inside the holding station waiting for night to fall. The birds rustled in the trees and rested on the branches overhead. Delicate chirps rang through the small holding area but held no mirth. Clouds shifted from visible shapes to thin traces in the sky, rotating the cold windy day into night. Far in the distance, I could hear the rumbling in the clouds somewhere and the loud chants of Muslim prayers. Thunder bolted. I knew the fine clusters of haze would gradually ascend, blending with the heavens above and that soon the nightfall and fog would give us the protection we needed to fly out. I was still feeling sluggish, and a small part of me didn't want to get on the helicopter.

My last talk with my roommate made me feel uneasy, but I was ready for my next adventure to Baghdad.

2000 hours

"Strap up! We're taking off!"

The female soldier held up two thumbs, while the other fiddled with a few switches above his head. This was my first time ever riding inside a helicopter. I'd heard horror stories about helicopters going down over land, over water. Scenes from the movie Black Hawk Downplayed over and over in my head.

"Okay," I replied and tried to smile. My fingers worked nervously as I manhandled the belt, secured myself, and popped in my earplugs. My heart beat rapidly as the strong gusts of wind from the blades above made my eyes water. I didn't know whether to foresee the ride as an exciting experience or to worry my heart into little pieces. I had always been told that most helicopters flying in a war didn't make it to their destinations. Hell, my roommate just warned me.

The helicopter began to sway from side to side. I could feel the nail-biting breeze shift from one side of my body and out of the doorless chopper. Though I appeared to be calm, there was a restless fire igniting in me—a fear so strong I began feeling sick. Every muscle in my body tensed, my world tilted, and I braced myself. "Just breathe and be calm," I repeated to myself. I could see the bare roots from the trees and our military vehicles began shrinking in size. The stars in the sky were appearing closer and closer, and the Fob was quickly disappearing.

The light from the moon passed through the inside of the chopper, and for a moment, I could see everything in detail. The sleek metal held all of our lives, offering us as a moving target through the sky. Safety harnesses dangled freely and rested in the empty seats. Wires hung from the top aimlessly with metal clasps banging against the steel walls. I could feel the thunder of the propellers in my chest, and the power of the engine hummed with every shift of the wind. I closed my eyes, and my thoughts began to swarm.

I kept thinking that the helicopter would stop in midair and then drop suddenly, killing us all. As the blades whopped in the air, I thought about how I should have called my mother one last time before I left. I thought about how different my life would have been if I didn't join and how I couldn't believe that I was in the middle of the Iraqi war. There I was, flying across Iraq. Everything seemed surreal.

Nearly 15 minutes had passed and I was still alive. I loosened up and tried to enjoy the ride. Opening my eyes periodically, I caught a glance of the female soldier in the front again. The color in my face had disappeared, and she motioned to me to calm down every time our eyes locked. I swallowed my smile and reconnected to my cynical feelings, remembering the conversation with my roommate a few hours before. I shook my head and closed my eyes. I couldn't control my thoughts: "I just want to hurry up and get there! Why did I join the Army?

This kind of stuff isn't for me. I should have never stopped going to college." The loud thudding of the blades thrashing through the winter winds continued to remind me of the old military movie Saving Private Ryan. I could feel every stroke in my heart, and every turn of this machine deep in my soul. I wanted to get off! Why did I have to get medically evacuated to Baghdad? What the hell was in my leg?

January 17, 2009

2030 hours Fob Kasul Karbala, Iraq

"Are you ready?" the female soldier asked with sobering eyes.

We had just landed in Fob Kasul, 20 miles south of Baghdad where Sunni Muslims made up most of the population.

"We are about to transfer you to another Black Hawk," the female soldier said again. "Make sure you have all of your gear. When I say move out, it's time to go. And make
sure you stay low."

Nearly a half a mile away, another helicopter waited as grains of dust whipped in the air. "Time to move out. Go, go, go!" she barked. I bobbed my head up and down, causing my bulletproof helmet called a Kevlar to shift.

I quickly unlocked my harness and got out of the helicopter. A few yards away, two different male soldiers huddled me back inside of a second helicopter and repeated for me to stay low until I got on board. Searching through the inside of the Black Hawk, I spied another soldier. His shoulders and head were dropped, and his mouth was moving, but I couldn't hear a single word. He looked young and terrified. I wanted to give him some comforting words, but the noise was just too loud. We made eye contact for a weak moment and I offered him a reassuring smile and a thumbs up with the hand that wasn't gripping the belt around my hips.

Gusty breaths of wind blew in and out of the chopper. The chill of the air was just as unwelcoming as the first ride, but I tried to enjoy the shifts of random currents in the atmosphere. My heart was just starting to slow to a somewhat peaceful thud when suddenly the helicopter dashed in the air as if it were losing control. We took a quick dart to the right and then a big dip. I was jolted forward, and my Kevlar shifted to the right side of my skull. I realized that we were in an area known for rockets and mortars shooting into the sky at passing helicopters and planes, and I screamed. I could see red lights coming toward our craft, and with every red light, the helicopter lurched to a different side, accelerating in speed. We dodged them all, but where were these flares coming from? And what were they?

CHAPTER 5.

BAGHDAD LIKE I'VE NEVER SEEN IT

2040 hours

Blinking, I knew for sure this was my end. This was it for me. We were going to be shot out of the night, be set loose, surrounded by hellish flames and left for dead. The young soldier let out a yelp. I looked around. Sitting back tightly in the chair, I threw my left leg out to compensate for the tilt of the helicopter. The angle of the machine grew and my gut knotted like a noose. I closed my eyes and my imagination ran wild. I imagined the helicopter landing hard, killing all aboard. I heard horrific screams drown out the noises from the helicopter blades. I saw metal and human remains scattered everywhere like a broken puzzle, bony thoraxes like the picked-over carcass from a Christmas pig, all white spine punctured from the hanging shreds of leftover skin. Ligaments still braided and ashes telling an inconceivable story. Snapping back to reality, I felt my heart in my throat, and I opened my eyes. All I could do was watch in agony and pray for the best, and hope that this damn flight would land in one piece. The red flares only lasted for a few seconds, but it seemed like an eternity.

2100 hours

We hovered over a city webbed with dim streetlights and palm trees. As we dropped lower, I could see buildings that looked like dusty gems. The air smelled much worse than Fob Echo's air. Here, I was sandwiched between the pungent smells of tar, hot fumigated oil, and sulfur. The air was hot and sat heavy in my chest. There was no escaping it out here. Still, it was better to be on the ground than high in the air, a moving target.

I arrived in Baghdad with a firm goal to never ride in a chopper again. Getting out of the craft, we were instructed to walk to the main entrance, check in, and wait for our next orders.

We headed north where there were signs with the word "emergency" on them. From the helicopter, I could see the hospital snaking around with large glass windows that glowed yellow and a sidewalk that forked in other directions. The dimness reminded me of the street lamps that would come on at night when I was a child playing outside. Every light in that hospital was on tonight.

"What the hell were those red flare things?" I said to the soldier as we picked up our speed. With our shoes slapping loud and as fast as popcorn, he replied.

"I don't know. But I thought we were gonna die."

His eyes sprang wide as they swept across our new destination.

Up ahead, a sliver of fluorescent light outlined the brown hospital's entrance and large conex storage containers laid scattered all around like Lego pieces near a row of sandy Humvees.

"I did too," I replied. "What were they? It looked like those things were coming right for us, didn't it?" With every step, I could still feel myself trembling like a Chihuahua.

"Yeah," he stammered.

Massive T-walls, man-made bunkers, and cinder blocks guarded this Fob. But beyond the manufactured protection, danger awaited us as the buildings exposed large rocket holes, shot Swiss-cheese-style yards away.

Inside the hospital, it felt meat-locker cold. I bought a few Snickers to snack on while I waited for my CT scan and watched the news as I sat in the waiting room. I never did find out what those red lights were, but I assumed the helicopter was being shot at. "Why didn't the people flying the helicopter seem scared of those flares?" I thought to myself. I thought it was strange that everyone went on his or her merry way. I wish I had spoken up, but I was spooked from that ride. I wanted to get far away from that helicopter.

2130 hours

The doctor glided over to me with confidence. The results for my CT scan images were locked in his hands. He ran his fingers through his short, blond hair and lifted his chin. He parted his lips then said my name.

"Benson." His breath smelled like Red Bull. "The CT isn't really revealing anything too major at this point," he said. "However, we're sending you to Germany to get an MRI. We could send you back to Echo, but it's better to be safe than sorry."

"As you can see," he continued, pointing to the images with his long bony index finger there. "There is blood flow here, so we can be sure of that. But that's all I can see from these images. We need to send you to Germany."

Germany? I thought. I didn't have much to say. What was I supposed to say? Here I was thinking that I'd only pulled a muscle in my leg. I managed to muster some scrambled words together.

"So... you don't know what it is?" I said.

The restless energy I had accumulated while I was on the helicopter cracked through my voice. I could hear the sound of boots tattooing the ground outside of the office room I was in, constantly interrupted by barking hurried orders. The doctor leaned forward, one elbow resting on his thigh. His eyes, full of understanding, calmed me down and I saw him in a new light. He was only trying to help and inform me.

"We need a more advanced test run in order to determine the current condition," he said. "This CT scan shows very little. This could be a number of things, but until we get the proper tests ran, we can't diagnose you, Benson."

He leaned back in his chair and his voice trailed off. Glancing to the corner of the room, he motioned a soldier with his finger as he rubbed his jaw anxiously with his other hand. I could hear him graze the stubble on his face.

"You're on the next flight smoking," he said.

My mind quickly linked the word flight to the horrible helicopter ride I'd just experienced. There was no way in hell I was going on another death ride.

"Flight? Do you mean flight as in airplane or helicopter?" My eyes were glazed over in fear.

"Neither, a C-130."

I pictured the four-engine aircraft and sighed. "Thank you, sir."

He replied with a nod and walked off. His tall silhouette disappeared into the doorway and then he was gone. I stayed back for further instructions from a specialist, feeling strangely relieved.

Most people, after traveling all this way and receiving no answers might feel apprehensive, but I remembered still thinking that it couldn't be all that bad. If it were something serious, if I was in any real danger, they would've found it by now. The doctor, after all, hadn't seemed worried.

2230 hours

After talking to the specialists and getting my new room key, I felt excited to see what the room might look like. The beds and living areas had to be better than the ones at Fob Echo. The upcoming trip to Germany had also lightened my mood. I hoped I'd get to stay there for a while, at least to go get a beer or something and be a tourist for a day or two. It had been a while since I drank a cold beer. Before this deployment, a glass of beer with a large head of foam wasn't a good thing. But right about now, just the very thought of the foam touching my lips and creating a beer mustache was delicious. You really never know how much you miss something until it's gone. I had been deprived of beer too long.

The hospital in Baghdad was well kept. The halls smelled like citrus and bleach. The fluorescent lights were bright and the walls were strong and sturdy as bones. I could even see my reflection on the hospital floors. It was a huge difference from Fob Echo in Iraq; Some of Fob Echo's rooftops were weak and bent or still under repair, the floors weren't ever this clean and the people burning the trash were miles away, but you could still see the smoke. I adjusted my shoestring as I walked down the hall to my new room and smiled. This was the perfect opportunity, I thought to myself. It was like a little vacation, and Germany would soon meet my feet. I had a smile on my face that only a plastic surgeon could remove.

Looking back on moments like these, I was so foolish. Being young and athletic my whole life really pulled the wool over my eyes and made me feel untouchable. I didn't smoke and I was constantly at the gym. I didn't think cancer was something that could happen to me. I thought only old or unhealthy people got cancer. I was wrong. I was happy though, that I was naive about it all. Knowing the way I would handle the news later when it finally came, I'm glad that I held on to those last few moments of happiness and didn't spend any time worrying over something I couldn't control.

CHAPTER 6.

GERMANY: MY SAFE HAVEN

January 20, 2009
0600 hours

I walked onto the C-130, took a seat, and fell right to sleep.

Rattle, rattle, rattle.

A commotion tore me out of my sleep, and I opened my eyes to see a burn victim in a gurney directly in front of me. His eyes were taped shut and dried blood clung to his lips like hungry leeches. The rise and fall of his chest was rapid, and parts of his face and stomach were raw with pebbles and inflamed festering boils.

I was on my way to Germany and had slept most of the flight. While I was passed out, we had stopped to pick up some IED victims and flew through a rainstorm. I had slept through all the turbulence and loud noises; I didn't even hear the machine that he was hooked up to. This wasn't like me, sleeping through a flight, but I was still feeling exhausted, greedily grabbing any seconds of sleep that I could.

I couldn't stop looking at the burned man. A large tube was snaking out of his mouth and leading up to a large machine. I stared at the tribal tattoo that coiled around his forearm past his elbow and marched up to his broad shoulder, ending in a heart with a woman's name. I felt so bad for him. This was someone's child, brother, uncle, or father. The machine continued to beep and pump air into his lungs, and a loud hiccup shook the aircraft. His battle buddy was below him in a gurney too, but he was dead. I gasped in shock and continued to stare as my eyes teared up.

This aircraft was huge, bigger than any other flight I have been on. The ceiling looked like a large dome, and there were no rows of seats. All the seats were pushed back to the sides where the windows should have been. In the middle, there were gurneys. A few were in use.

There were no nice warnings from the cockpit telling us that we were expecting turbulence, or nice men and women walking up and down the aisle with peanuts and refreshment. When the craft shook like the world was ending, no one made a sound to warn us. Everyone just grabbed their seat belts and adjusted them tighter.

January 20, 2009
0800 hours Landstuhl, Germany

Walking off of the plane, I could see the hospital here in Germany. I could also see gigantic trees towering above—trees that shot to the sky like dandelions and others that bowed back down to the ground. Getting off the plane, I noticed a thin slice of the moon still up from the night before. Luckily, we had missed the rainstorm. The angry rain had calmed to a spell of drops and dawn was approaching quickly. The dew gathered on the grass, making it look like sparkling stars had fallen from the sky and landed perfectly on each strand. The frail sunlight reflected off the wet grass and maintained a sheer reflection on the busy street. As I rounded the bend, I caught my first glance of real hope.

There it was, the real hospital, with real help and real equipment. I felt secure; I felt like this was the end of the road and that all my questions would soon have answers.

I boarded a white bus and headed off to the hospital. As we drove, the rain tapped the top of the bus like sliding loose pebbles. I looked around and everyone seemed to be in bad shape, all requiring major medical attention. Some soldiers were in casts—arms, legs, feet, and torsos.

Walking off the bus, I could hear the birds squawking, the loud hiss of the engine behind me and soldiers cackling. We were all handed a manila folder with our first and last name on it. Our names were called off by a non-commissioned officer shortly after.

"Benson!" A male liaison shouted out. His small eyes grazed our tiny group of broken soldiers. I looked up at the fair-skinned man with a uniform that matched mine. Soggy leaves wrestled with each other on the ground as the breeze cupped their wilted frames, causing them to spin and dance limply.

"Yes, sergeant," I said. "That's me."

The non-commissioned officer then waved me toward him. As he exhaled, small warm breaths of air slowly disappeared into the wet sky. Wiping the rain off of his nose, he barked out the rest of the names, as the icy raindrops dripped off the edge of the paper. Standing next to him, I couldn't help but to gaze at the scenery again. My breath was lost somewhere deep inside my lungs, and I was still amazed that I was actually in Germany. I had learned so much back in the states about Hitler, and I couldn't wait to call my mom and let her know that I was here.

"Benson, you will be on the fourth floor. That's where all the females are." He pointed to a building on a little hill. "That's where you will be for your duration, soldier. Inside this folder are the directions. Now move it."

"Yes, sergeant." I moved out as I was told.

The building ahead was four stories tall and newly renovated with glass windows. The grass was green and evenly cut throughout the entire terrain, and a black steel gate lined the circumference of the post. My temporary home was room 416.

"It's great to be in a clean country and have fresh air," I said to myself. Holding my bags firmly, I shuffled over to the structure. Soldiers were walking

THE ENEMY INSIDE ME 57

about by the dozens, laughing in the rain. Others stood by the designated smoke pits puffing away and spitting in the far corners. I didn't see any signs of heightened tension or nervous conversations. There weren't any bunkers or T-walls. I didn't see any soldiers walking around with their weapons, and no one was wearing their bulletproof vest or Kevlars. I didn't even see any empty shell cases anywhere. The trash cans weren't even full to the brim with Red Bulls or Rip It drinks. Instead, I saw fast food bags. The air was even lighter.

It was a great feeling to see soldiers not worried about the next mortar hitting or war in general. The manila folder I clasped contained all my upcoming appointments, a map of the military installation, the key to my room, and a gift certificate for $200 for the military store here on base.

0900 hours

My first appointment was the MRI. I had traveled over many countries just to find an answer. The day was still alive and full of adventure; nightfall wouldn't be setting anytime soon.

I decided to give my mom a call. The last thing she knew was that I was still in Iraq. I needed to catch her up on a few things and my new destination.

I was amazed to see no lines at the telephones. The room was bright and had its own little cubicle for privacy. Fob Echo always had a huge line meandering around the corner and zigzagging through the call center, but here in Germany, I didn't have to worry about that. There was no one in line. I could call as many people as I wanted without worrying about my time running out, getting attacked and having to fight for the phone, or dealing with 24-hour communication blackouts. When you did make a phone call back to the states, you had to use a calling card or a personal cell phone. Either way, you were waiting in line to purchase the calling card or to make a phone call. But here, there was none of that. No calling cards needed or long depressing lines. I felt like Germany was going to be a great vacation, and when I returned back to Fob Echo, I would be rejuvenated.

Walking to my own cubicle, I picked up the tan phone, dialed 99, then my mother's number. Outside of the window, I could see a small red squirrel resting in the candy corn colored leaves, and a pack of grey birds knifing through the air. Here, in Germany, I was six or seven hours ahead of Texas. I knew my mother would be up, running around the house packing Donavin's diaper bag and getting ready for work. She had to get up every day at 0500 hours. to drop him off at the babysitter's across town, then drive all the back to work at the hair salon she managed. She was a busy lady but always made time to talk to her kids, no matter how tired she was.

1300 hours

Ring, ring, ring.

"Hello?" A soft voice said, splintered with curiosity. I could hear Donavin in the background mumbling words. In the same breath, my mother asked him if he wanted more juice.

"Ma, it's Brandi," I said.

"Brandi?" she called. "Where are you calling me from, I don't recognize the number." I laughed a bit as my heart filled with joy, and I coiled the phone cord around my finger.

My mother repeated the question to Donavin. "Do you want more juice or water, baby?"

I sat quietly on the phone waiting to hear what Donavin answered. Like a chime, a small voice said, "Wawa."

I smiled and quickly grabbed my mother's attention. "Ma, you won't even believe it," I said. "I'm in Germany."

My mother cleared her throat and the refrigerator peeled open. "Why are you in Germany? Is everything okay?"

I wanted to break down and cry to her, to tell her that I was scared. It was a feeling that had come out of nowhere. But scared of what? I hadn't even been diagnosed. The doctors weren't even sure what I had. Even though something deep inside me made me want to break down, I threw a quick tone of bravery into my voice.

"Yes," I replied. "I'm here because I need to get an MRI for my leg. I think I pulled a muscle. I have this bump in my leg."

"A bump?" my mother asked and I heard water being poured. "Where is it?"

After years of watching me go to the hospital for various minor reasons, I didn't expect my mom to be concerned. Growing up, I definitely wasn't your average pretty princess girl. I was a huge tomboy. I broke many bones playing basketball, sprained nearly every muscle in my legs and had stitches from cuts, and gashes from falling out of trees or rollerblading down steep dangerous hills. I expected learning that I was in Germany to get an MRI for what I thought was a pulled muscle was no surprise to her. I heard her sigh into the phone receiver.

"You're always in the hospital, Brandi," she said then called for Donavin to come over. "Where did you say you pulled the muscle again?"

"It's in my left leg near my groin area," I said. "I've been training really hard at the gym for about a month now, and I'm sure I just tweaked something."

"That seems a bit strange don't you think, Brandi?" Her tone was laced with the daunting realization that this was more than what I thought. "You've pulled a lot of muscles growing up, and you never had to get an MRI. Have you?"

She was right. I had been in and out of several emergency rooms for sprains, broken bones, pulled muscles and cuts, but none required an MRI. Sure, I got the regular x-rays, but no MRI. Even then, after hearing my mother's voice change from nonchalant to a concerned parent, I ignored the clues.

"No," I replied and locked my eyes on the floor. "No, I haven't, but what else could it be?"

She didn't have an answer, but before getting off the phone, my mother reassured me that everything was going to be okay.

"Just wait to see what the doctors have to say," she said. "I'm sure there's nothing to worry about, but you better call me once you know something."

I promised her I would.

That night a mixture of emotions kept me awake. A part of me was so excited to be in Germany at a better base, which meant better food and a better gym and more time to sleep. But another part of me started to worry about what my mother had said. She had raised a valid question, and I didn't have a response. As I sat in bed, I looked at my body, tracing every scar with my fingers and trying to remember if I'd ever had an MRI or a CT scan before. I came up short.

I thought back to Iraq and all the people who seemed to be more worried about my situation than I was: my roommate, my workout buddy, and now my mother. I tried to imagine what I would do if the lump turned out to be something serious, possibly deadly, but I couldn't. It didn't seem possible. Denial took over once again and I shrugged it off.

"It couldn't be anything else," I said to myself. I just knew that nothing was wrong.

CHAPTER 7.

RESULTS AND KARMA

January 22, 2009
0800 hours

I awoke early the next morning in Germany, jumping out of my pajamas, into my uniform and out of the door. As I walked through the grey morning headed to the hospital, excitement throbbed through my curious body, competing with my new constant exhaustion. I was still tired (always tired), but I was more anxious, ready to finally know what was going on. The rain from the night before had finally stopped, making the ground soft like pillows beneath my feet. The sidewalk jogged to the right a bit and ended at the black steel gate where a man stood tall and proud. He introduced himself with a shy, gapped-tooth smile.

"Good morning, sir," I said.

"Young lady," he nodded his head. "Identification please." The words ran around in my head for a few seconds. I was so damn tired that even a simple conversation took too much energy. My eyes narrowed into the small gaps in his teeth.

"Ma'am, I can't let you through the gate unless you identify yourself."

"Oh, yeah, ID," I said, snapping out of it. "Right. ID. Where did I put it?" Scrambling in my pockets I pulled out an old Snickers wrapper. "No, that's not it. One second, sir. I'm sure I have it." My fingers finally made contact with the ID in my pocket. "Found it. Here you are, sir."

I held out my military card with my left hand. As the gate opened up, I shoved the ID back into my right pocket. There it was. The hospital. The hammering in my heart sped up a few beats.

"Thank you, sir. Have a great day." His eyes narrowed and his expression made my stomach do a sinuous roll inside my belly. Thinking back at this moment, I feel like my intuition was trying to tell me something and that's why I felt sick when I locked eyes with the man at the gate. But of course, I ignored all the signs. Holding onto the handle of the gate, I closed my eyes, drew in a long shaky breath, and proceeded to my final destination: the MRI waiting room.

0845 hours

The waiting room had small chairs pushed against the polished glass windows. The room boasted a few pine tables that held outdated magazines and a TV high up in a corner to the left. The bland curtains on the windows hung low and matched the cushions on the chairs. Off to the far left was a station with freshly brewed coffee, sugar, and tea. The whispers of the television were quiet and comforting.

"Benson." The words echoed through my hollow body and my muscles jolted in anticipation. It was the guy at the desk. I looked up to see a short soldier scanning the room.

"Benson," I said pointing to myself. "Come this way please."

Leading me to a cold empty room, he handed me a neatly folded hospital gown, along with a box of yellow cashew-sized earplugs. He gave no further instructions, but I was sure what to do. At Superman speed, I changed and led myself to a small narrow table. With my hips swaying from side to side, I could feel the frosty air rising up my legs with every stride. The free strings that hung from my gown kissed the back of my thighs gently with every step I took. I sat down and waited.

There was a soft knock at the door and it eased open.

"How are you doing, Benson?" said the MRI tech. He continued without waiting for an answer. "Alright, so. We're focusing on the left leg?" Breaking eye contact with the orders he had in a vice grip, he stared at my legs.

"Yes, it's my left inner leg, by my groin area."

"Okay, what I need you to do, Benson, is put those earplugs in and lay down on here." He motioned me in like he was directing traffic.

Inside this loud, cramped machine, I was reminded of a tight chamber that I saw at Ginnie Springs in Florida on a video about scuba diving. The divers swam through tight, small passageways the same size as this tunnel I was in. With only a six-inch gap of space, I began feeling claustrophobic. All I could see were white walls and a red laser that scanned me. The lack of ventilation made me uneasy. With my arms close to my sides, I felt like I was breathing in my own carbon dioxide instead of fresh air. As the machine banged and rattled, only getting louder and filling my ears despite the earplugs, it finally dawned on me. A moment of panic surprised me, and out of nowhere, I was actually feeling a bit scared for the first time. Going over the doctors' responses from the last few days, I began understanding that something must be really wrong. This could be, and probably was, more than just a pulled muscle. It could possibly be an infection or a cyst. Cancer never crossed my mind.

1700 hours

I called my mother as I had promised, and talked to her all night. With laughter in her voice, she told me how funny Donavin was getting, and how he was looking more and more like my sister. I explained my concerns with the MRI and how I was feeling a bit uneasy about it all. She reassured me that everything was going to be okay and to wait for the results. We talked about Germany and Hitler, the chocolate candies and the gummy bears here, we talked about how old the place looked, then ended our conversation with an "I love you."

CHAPTER 8.

IN OVER MY HEAD AND TURNING TO GOD

January 25, 2009
0800 hours

Three days after my MRI, I sat back in the waiting room of the hospital, glancing at the television. In the glass, I could see a slight reflection of the zombie soldiers and myself. Through the window in front of me, soldiers waited in the hall. Some of the soldiers had mouths full of chewing tobacco. Others held a hot ceramic coffee cup to their lips. Sports scores dribbled across the TV screen and the nonsense of loose jargon nested in my ears.

Minutes later, I was led to the same room as before. I was here to see the same doctor who had previously given me the MRI exam and to find out the results.

"Hello, doctor," I spoke up first. I had decided to skip the pleasantries and get him straight to the point. "Have you found out what the lump is?"

He gazed at me, a long and sorrowful look before

he spoke. The morning sun cast feeble rays across his square jaw, and I could see sparkles of sweat collecting on the bridge of his tiny nose. Not a single strand of hair was out of place. Sharing a sad boyish smile with me, he gently placed his hand on my left knee, causing me to shiver. I hadn't been touched in a tender way since I joined the Army. No hugs or pats on the back, only the cold hands of a doctor poking at my flesh or the rough hands of a fellow soldier holding my feet to the floor while I forced my body to do just one more sit up.

"Yes," he said in a whisper, almost as if he didn't want me to hear him. The room fell into a dead silence as I waited. I could now hear the lub-dub in my heart. His eyes were glazed and the little drops of sweat began to grow in size. He seemed nervous, not confident.

Hitching my chin a fraction, I found myself staring into his grey, puppy eyes that matched the steel I sat on. Lapping my tongue around my cotton-dry lips, I felt faint.

"It's a tumor."

The word "tumor" dropped out of his mouth like a weight. It landed at my feet and sat there, waiting on me to accept and understand it, but I didn't. It was as if I'd never heard it before. He kept talking as I tried to catch up. It was a fact that was too hard to swallow.

"We have to get a biopsy of the mass. This will determine the type of tumor it is. It could be malignant or benign. Either way, you will have to get it surgically removed."

"I have a tumor," I said. It wasn't really a question, not yet. I simply formed the words in my mouth, still trying to catch up with this new information. My eyes were untamed with terror, and my body was as cold as December. I felt like a hostage in my own body.

"Are you sure?"

"Yes, Benson. Go to the reception area and get the appointment for your biopsy." "Will do, sir," I replied dryly, and, like a ghost, I glided out of the room.

Walking to the reception area, everything seemed so surreal. The walls of the hallway looked different, the lights were too bright, and I had to squint my eyes. My mouth was so dry.

I had a "tumor" in my body.

I was and always will be a firm believer in karma. As I walked down to the reception area, I couldn't help but wonder what I had done to deserve this. Had I been a bad person?

Names of people from my past appeared in my mind as I tried to remember what our relationships were like and if I'd harmed them in any way or left any bad blood behind me. I cataloged through the names of neighbors, classmates, forgotten family members, childhood friends, searching for something awful that I'd done that was terrible enough to cause a tumor in my leg. I came up empty-handed.

Then different names started to appear, accompanied by flashes of memory, the smell of smoke, and the feeling of sticky floors. Cherry, with her long blonde hair, toned arms and legs, walking across a stage in red pumps. Luscious, at the bar ordering a drink, already scanning the crowd for the next customer. Kitty, in all pink with full brown locks of hair shading the glassy expression in her eyes. Half-naked women were everywhere, perky-breasted brunettes and blondes, long hair and short hair, round butts and long torsos, manicured feet, and hands, glittered and perfumed, pouty red and pink lips. I shook my head in an effort to make the memories disappear. No, I thought. That can't be it. I was just there to make a quick buck.

July 3, 2003

1200 hours

Hawaii By Night Gentlemen's Club Honolulu, Hawaii

There were two dancers in front of me dancing on the lit-up stage. The stage was flashing green and yellow lights along the edge; they kind of looked like Christmas lights. Two girls were on stage together. One girl was snapping her long silky straight hair from side to side as her thin legs pointed toward the mirrors on the ceiling. The other brunette, Kitty, twirled on the pole like a ballerina then stopped and pointed her finger to me by the stage. She did the universal sign with her finger for "come here".

Motley Crue's, "Girls, Girls, Girls" was playing loud. Another dancer walked past the stage dressed in babydoll lingerie. The baby doll dancer pranced around with a thin cigarette in her hand and little red Os on the end of her cigarette butt. Baby doll's boobs were so big that I bet that her feet didn't get wet when she showered.

I walked over to Kitty with my hands in my pockets.

"How much more do you want?" I yelled loud against the bass in the music. "An eight- ball or what?" Boom, boom, boom, boom.

The bass was vibrating in my throat and I could feel it in my feet. The speaker next to me boomed so loud that the glass on top shook.

Kitty looked at me with her pupils the size of saucers and grinded her teeth back and forth.

"Yeah, let me get a little bump first." She never broke character, continuing to dance while she talked to me. A man threw some dollar bills from the other side of the stage as she twisted her rump in a circle. The money fell to the ground like confetti.

"Okay, I'll meet you in the bathroom again."

Crawling slowly, Kitty took the money and slid it to the corner. Laying on her perfectly sculpted abs, she propped herself with her elbows and squashed her breasts together.

"I'll be right back," she said to her new customer, who was now reaching into his pants to move more things than his cash and car keys.

Women hung from the ceiling like apples dangling from a tree. The scarlet lights erased any blemishes and the black light made the dancer's eyes glow. The whole place seemed more exotic with the lights flashing. It was like a fantasy until I met Kitty in the bathroom with its harsh fluorescent lights, urine-soaked toilet paper scattered on the ground, and a clogged drain in the middle of the floor.

The lights were on and I could see Kitty as well as myself. I was 18 and this was my first real job: a cocktail waitress/drug dealer.

I opened up the baggie, tapped the bag a few times, and drew a line with the powder.

Kitty bent at the waist, squeezed one nostril, then stopped.

"Is this the last of it?" Her voice is muffled near the bathroom counter. "No, I have as much as you want," I replied. Kitty sniffed hard and loud.

It wasn't something I wanted to do, and often I found myself looking in the cracked bathroom mirror of the club, squeezing the sides of the sink and telling myself not to cry and to get back out there. A few months before I started, my stepdad had left my mother after 14 years of marriage. He left her with all the bills, three dogs, and two kids. Every month, something was getting turned off. First, it was the TV, then the house phone. Then we didn't have enough food to feed the dogs, and then we didn't have enough to feed ourselves. Soon we were late on rent and faced eviction. I was old enough to realize that someone needed to do something. I made my mind up to find a job—something that would make fast money.

I didn't work there long, but the faces of those women, the smell of that place, and the arrogant pride that came along with making so much money that young stayed with me for a long time.

Just like my religious preference, the choices I made stemmed from many years ago, but my reasons were more than legit. Some years later when asked about religion, and if I thought I was going to hell for selling drugs to strippers, made me wonder if this cancer was my karma.

Often as an adult, I would think about that time in my life and wonder how I'd found myself there. It'd be easy to say that I'd been innocent and found myself there accidentally. It'd be easy to claim I didn't realize the error of my ways, but none of that is true. What is true is that I was only 18 and my job made me feel like a grown woman, in control and on top of the world.

I was raised as a Christian. I went to bible study groups as a good little Christian kid does. I attended The Lord's Church in Novato, California; this is where I lived most of my younger years before I moved to Hawaii at the age of 16 and the state that I was born. It was big, but not too big, with one whole wall dedicated to pictures of Jesus Christ and a large crucifix. The windows were stained glass and shone of gold, red and green.

I hated church as a young girl, and I found it to be more scary than helpful. I never felt the peace I was supposed to find there. I didn't find it amusing that people fell to the ground shaking and crying and claiming that the Holy Spirit got to them. It scared me when someone who was perfectly normal outside of the church, suddenly turned from English-speaking people to people who spoke in tongues. Church, to me, felt like a cage, but my fear of going to hell kept me securely locked inside until September 22, 1992.

On September 22, 1992, Pastor Dan Elledge was murdered inside my church. Mexican thugs gunned him down in The Lord's Church—a robbery gone wrong. My aunt Maria got a phone call, sat me down, and told me the horrible news. I was beyond shocked. The thought of death petrified me, especially in a place that was supposed to belong to the Lord. This was the day I lost all my faith in Christianity. I realized church was like any other place and that it would be better to just stay home. The change in my behavior was immediately noticeable. Instead of believing in one almighty, I worshipped the God of hustling, working hard, and getting what you want. The fear of hell still lingered, but now it was peppered with the fear of failure and torture on Earth. I now knew those bad things could happen anywhere to anyone.

"What's your religion?" Kitty always asked me, and never seemed to understand why or how I came to this decision. I never explained it to her; it was none of her business.

"Agnostic," was always my quick and safe answer.

Being agnostic didn't blind me from the bad I was doing at the strip club. I wasn't completely fooled by the flashing lights and quick money. I never thought about karma or God while I worked there. I knew right from wrong and was smart enough to know that if it had to be categorized, selling drugs to strippers was definitely wrong.

But I also knew what it was like to watch your mother cry over bills in the kitchen, then watch her face break into a smile when you hand her a stack of sweaty money, saying, "It's yours." It felt a lot like God. My mother knew I was a cocktail waitress but didn't know the real truth behind it. I couldn't dare tell her the truth. I couldn't break her heart again. I couldn't let her down.

January 25, 2009
0900 hours

But now, standing in the reception room of a cold hospital, I felt like God had finally come to remind me that I wasn't in control, and I wasn't on top of the world. I placed my hand on my leg and mumbled the word "tumor" again and again. The feeling of uncertainty became stronger. What if those religious people were right all along? And I am the one in the wrong? Is this punishment? This had to be my lesson. This had to be it. I had turned away from God, if for only a moment, and now God was turning away from me.

2000 hours

I had to talk to my mom. Somehow I managed to drag myself to the calling area. My body felt like it was on autopilot. Step by step, one foot in front of the other, I reached out to grabbed the phone.

As the phone rang, I sat numbly and stared out of the window, not really seeing anything.

Even now I didn't think about the word "cancer." Instead, I thought about everything my mom had on her plate. With my sister also deployed, my mom was watching my nephew Donavin and taking care of all my sister's bills for her until she returned. Now I had to tell her the bad news. I thought about what it would be like to have surgery, being put under, something going wrong on the operating table. I wondered if I would have a large scar and if I'd be able to run anymore. The very thought of cancer never played a part in my thoughts.

I snapped out of my foggy head and realized the phone wasn't ringing anymore. "Hello?" my mom said on the other end. "What did the doctor say, Brandi?"

I could hear the anxiety in her voice. I held my breath for a few seconds then shook my head back and forth. I couldn't even believe what I was about to tell her.

"The doctor said I have a tumor." There was a small pause, just a beat.

"A tumor? What do you mean, Brandi?"

My heart began to swell, feeling too big for my chest. My mom was still talking.

"Brandi … Do you hear me? What kind of tumor is it?"

"I don't know," I said, my mouth dry. "They didn't say. I have to get a biopsy of it." "Brandi, how do you not know?" I recognized her take-charge tone immediately and steeled myself. "God, I wish I were there with you. Are you asking the right questions?"

I didn't know what to say. What could I tell her? All I wanted was to go to sleep as soon as possible. I felt weighed down with exhaustion.

"Ma, I am asking the right questions," I snapped back when she said my name again. "They can't tell me anything until I get the biopsy. Ma, do you think it's cancer?"

A long paused elapsed, and I knew my mother was reliving the same memories from my grandfather.
"No, there's just no way. Don't think like that. Everything will be okay."

When I got back to my room, I took four Benadryl and let the anxiety in my mind dissolve like sugar mixed into water. I was soon asleep and would wake up to a whole different life.

CHAPTER 9.

NEVER TOO SICK TO PLAY GAMES

January 26, 2009
1130 hours

The next day at my biopsy, my MRI tech came to where I was. I offered a friendly smile and he moved in closer. I could see the sweat breaching out of his scalp as he shuffled the results back and forth with his hands, which were lumpy with veins.

"The mass is a Nerve Sheath tumor, but it might be Ewing Sarcoma." His skin was spotted with red and brown spots.

I could only nod my head and try to understand what was being said to me. It was like watching a Spanish movie and I only knew a few words.

"If we know what kind of tumor it is, then why do I have to do this biopsy?"

Over his horn-rimmed glasses, he looked at me with a very stern and sour expression as if he'd just tasted vinegar.

"Young lady, this is going to determine the exact

type," he told me. "The images from the MRI show two similar cases of tumors. It could be a Nerve Sheath tumor or Ewing Sarcoma. I just hope it's not Ewing Sarcoma."

A younger lady in her mid-twenties with raven black hair came from around the corner. Her hands were clad in green gloves and a cheerless smile toyed with her pink lips. She walked over hesitantly and pulled out an 18-gauge needle. "Which arm?" she asked. I flopped out my left arm.

"Okay, now you're just going to feel a little prick," she said, as she stuck the needle in my arm. She explained that I needed to have an IV started so that the contrast would allow the area on my leg to light up while I was in the MRI. Doing this would help them target the mass and get the images they needed. Her voice trailed off and she drew her mouth shut as the machine began to make loud knocking noises.

January 30, 2009
0800 hours

Today, I received the results from my biopsy. The night before, I did some research on tumors. A Nerve Sheath tumor can form in the peripheral nerve network anywhere in the body. The majority of those tumors are noncancerous—majority meaning that there was a possibility it was cancerous. Ewing Sarcoma, the type of tumor my doctor had hoped out loud I didn't have, is a malignant small, round, blue cell tumor, which typically represents a number of neoplasms that have the same characteristic appearance under the microscope. The predominance of blue staining is due to the fact that the cells consist predominantly of the nucleus; thus they have scant cytoplasm, scant cytoplasm is the material within a living cell. It is a rare disease in which cancer cells are found in the bone or in soft tissue and the death rate is high.

This tumor spreads to the bones, the lungs, and the brainstem. At that point, you might as well throw in the towel and consider yourself dead. With Ewing Sarcoma, you're just a walking accelerated expiration date. Those tumors are found mostly in young Caucasian boys, which gave me a slight moment of relief. Then I remembered when I first noticed the lump on my leg and chalked it up to a pulled muscle. I was wrong once, and I could be wrong again. I kept wondering what I would do if I had cancer. Not how I would react in the doctor's office, but how I would react for the rest of my life? What would I do? How would I spend the time I had left in my life? How do I qualify that time?

After researching, I cried. I cried all night. I cried about leaving my mother. I cried about not being able to watch my nephew grow up. I hoped that I had the Nerve Sheath because it seemed like the lesser of the two evils. Then I cried about having to prefer a type of cancer. I cried about everything.

I reached out to the God I'd shrugged off years ago. I begged that the lump was only a Nerve Sheath Tumor. I promised to take religion more seriously.

Through my sobs, runny nose, and swollen eyes, I pleaded all night.

"God, I promise to live a better life. I won't drink anymore. I'll even go on missions like those crazy Mormons. Wait, I take it back. They aren't crazy. They are smart! I'll go door to door spreading the word. Just, please. I don't want cancer!" I could only wish that my prayers were sent up FedEx style and that my request didn't get denied.

0730 hours

The following morning, my eyes were puffy, shoulders hunched, head bowed. I carried myself with insecurity down the familiar halls. I made it to the same doctor's office and waited for him to arrive with my results. I sat on a table, and nearly 15 minutes later he appeared. He walked in slowly.

"This might be hard to take," he cleared his throat. "It's cancer, but that doesn't mean you're going to die. We're sending you to Walter Reed Medical Center, where they can treat you. Chemotherapy will help you." Everything began to slow down and I became dizzy. I balled up my fists and considered telling the doctor that I'd heard those words before. I'd heard them drenched with disbelief and sorrow from the mouth of my grandmother. My mind flashed back to that patio outside. I thought about his grave. I thought about his wife, my grandmother.

July 15, 2004
0900 hours
Honolulu, Hawaii

My grandfather was cremated, leaving only a picture of him in his police uniform to pay our respects at his funeral. Men, women, and children were all dressed in their best. The men wore suits, aloha shirts, and creased slacks. Their shoes were polished and their outfits complemented their freshly shaved faces. Women wore long elegant dresses, necklaces that countered their matching earrings, and beautiful flowers nested in their hair. The young boys and girls all wore similar outfits, the only difference being a few ketchup stains. After the funeral, we all went back to my aunt's house in Honolulu.

My aunt's house was packed that day. Cars occupied her diminutive driveway and soon made their way to the yard. Cars by the dozen were lined up in the grass, and the zigzags of passing feet led to the doorway.

Inside, were a plethora of snacks: cheese and crackers, hamburgers and hot dogs, chips and dip, veggie trays and fruit trays, kalua pork and poi, fried fish and chicken, and juice and soda. The home was buzzing with people. Groups of people scattered about, just eating, talking, and crying.

My grandmother took it the hardest. She sat where my grandfather had sat just a few days before.

As she sat there, wiping the tears from her face, she abruptly shouted out things in the direction of the sparkling sea ahead of us. She cried, she begged. She damned cancer and she cursed the world.

We all stole peeks of her from the inside of the

house but then, embarrassed or unsure what to do, tucked our chins down — the look of submission. It's the look when we feel so sorry for someone that we don't dare make eye contact. Instead, we stared endlessly at that damn floor.

Her bursts of sobs got continuously louder and eventually couldn't be ignored. Soon the entire inside of the house was staring at the floor. It was so quiet that I could hear the hissing from my soda can. We were hesitant to look up and meet her eyes from across the way, scared to look up and have to attempt to answer any of her questions. Months ago, we were all hopeful that the chemotherapy was going to save him. The doctors sold us the dream that he had a great fighting chance. She seemed to suddenly be out of words and folded over into wailing heaves. I placed my soda on the counter inside and headed to my grandmother who was balled up and crying like a child.

January 30, 2009
0801 hours

"I promise that everything is going to be okay, Benson," the doctor said as he placed his hand on me again.

I shook my head from side to side as the roaring in my ears became louder. I'd heard this exact same phrase just years before, for this same disease, and it hadn't played out well. It not only hurt to hear those words again, but it made me immediately distrust him. I was suddenly filled with an irrational hate for this man, born out of confusion, isolation, loneliness, despair, hopelessness—all the things I couldn't allow myself to feel in that moment. So I felt hate instead. I opened my mouth to speak.

"Everything is going to be okay?" I replied sarcastically. I let out a short dry laugh, one quick breath of air forced from my mouth. Then I started to yell at him.

"No, sir. I'm pretty sure you have the wrong results in your hands!" I shouted. "My name is Brandi. Brandi Benson. Look, I'm sure you have the wrong person!"

I didn't know how to stop myself from this outburst and the silent and accepting look on his face while I yelled only made me angrier.

"This can't be right!" I continued. "I am only 24! How could I have cancer?"

With that last question, I stopped yelling and looked down at the floor. My heartfelt too big for my chest. I was all by myself, with no family or friends to lean on.

CHAPTER 10.

MAKING DEALS

January 30, 2009
1500 hours

I don't remember leaving the hospital or walking into the calling room, but soon the phone was ringing in my hand.

Ring, ring, ring.

As soon as she picked up the receiver, I started wailing.

"What is it, Brandi?" she asked and I could hear the panic in her voice. "Brandi, what is it?"

I sniffed loudly and put my hand over my head. I was sweating. "I have cancer. Mom, I'm going to die!" The hysteria in her voice only made my tears come faster. She was wailing, a low sound that took a while to recognize as a word, one word. "Noooo!"

She was so loud, the guy in the cubicle next to me was staring as my mom continued to cry on the other end of the phone. "No, Brandi. Noooo!"

We both cried on the phone for what seemed like an eternity before she was able to speak again.

"Brandi, where are they sending you?" she demanded. "I am coming. I am leaving everything here. I am leaving everything and I am coming. I am quitting my job. Where are they sending you?"

My body shuddered and I could barely catch my breath. I knew I should've told her not to quit her job, not to worry, that the Army would take care of it and take care of me. But I needed nothing more than to see her.

"They're sending me to Walter Reed Medical Center in Washington, D.C.," I replied.

"Brandi," my mom said, still catching her breath and sniffing. "This isn't the end, okay?" Her voice was nasally and high. "We have to stay positive. You're going to beat this thing!"

Getting off the phone, I noticed the guy next to me was crying. I would later find out that he had just lost his brother to lung cancer.

"Ma'am," he said shyly, nodding his head in a gentlemanly way as if he'd just removed a hat in my presence. "Do you believe in God?"

March 26, 2009

1700 hours

Walter Reed Medical Center, Washington, D.C.

"How are you feeling, Brandi?" my mother asked while we sat in my hospital room.

My mom shuffled the deck of cards in front of us on my hospital table, keeping one eye on the cards and one worried eye on my face. With her thumb on one of the short ends and the rest of her fingers on the other side, she curled her index finger and pushed down on it. She shuffled like a professional who works Blackjack in Las Vegas.

"Remember, if you feel sick, just call the doctor and they will give you that medicine to make you feel better, okay?"

I was on my fifth cycle of chemotherapy and really feeling the symptoms badly. I couldn't go anywhere without being chauffeured around in a wheelchair. If I did walk somewhere, after 50 feet, my heart felt like a revving Hennessey Venom GT. My hair was already falling out by clumps and the smell of my urine when I went to the bathroom made me gag. There were other symptoms too, ones nobody ever tells you about. The tips of my fingers were always tingly like they had fallen asleep and I could no longer write legibly. The muscles in my hands were so weak that even holding a pen was too hard.

She shuffled the cards once more and the cards popping against each other reminded me of an icemaker.

"You know you have to eat something," she continued. "The doctors said you have to maintain your weight." Her voice was measured and frank as she sat the cards to the side.

"Here, drink this," she said and pushed an Ensure closer to me.

But I couldn't eat anything and she knew that. I

hadn't had an appetite in days. I felt myself fall into a deeper depression every day. People kept telling me to be positive, but knowing that this was just the beginning of chemotherapy made me irritable. My optimism dwindled away as fast as my looks and my sense of self. I kept feeling like I'd wake up one morning and, like Dorothy in the Wizard of Oz, I'd rub my eyes and think, "What an awful dream!"

But it wasn't a dream. This was my new reality.

"I don't have an appetite," I told my mom through gritted teeth, not bothering to raise my gaze to meet hers. I knew she would have that worried look on her face. "I just don't feel well at all."

We were playing rummy while we passed the time waiting for my sister to arrive from Iraq. I hadn't seen my sister in nearly a year at her basic training graduation. Proud tears rolled down my cheeks as I watched her graduate.

Now, nearly a year later, I would be crying not tears of joy but tears of fear.

We were supposed to meet in Hawaii for our R&R at the end of March, but my stay in the hospital derailed our plans. Instead, Michelle would stay with me, and my mom and Donavin would stay in her room for the two weeks of R&R.

1900 hours

The door eased open and the hinges let out a soft, quiet sigh. It was my sister, Michelle. My mother and I sat up, and I walked to her. The large lump in my leg was shrinking due to the chemotherapy, but I still couldn't fully extend my leg. I hobbled over to my sister with my left leg halfway bent. She was wearing a big black fleece and blue jeans. With Michelle's arms wide open, I flew toward her and fell into her arms. I cried and I cried and I cried. I released every ounce of worry and fear I'd been trying to hold back in front of my mother. Michelle set her bags to the ground and cradled my head.

"Everything is going to be okay, Brandi," she said as squeezed me. Her fleece smelled like oil and dust. It was the same oil and fumes that engulfed me a few weeks ago in Iraq.

"She must be next to the burn pits, too," I thought to myself.

The evening sunlight bled through the curtains and gave the room a warm glow against the fluorescent lights in my room. The vertical shadows swayed side to side from the gust of air that pushed through the door. Outside of my window, the world continued on. Cars zoomed by in the crisp, cold air. Buses put out grey mushrooms of smoke. People shuffled around with their plastic grocery bags, and taxies darted through traffic with demanding passengers. And here I was, with bloodshot eyes and a runny nose, embracing my sister for what could be the last time.

Michelle and I looked at each other, and she smiled. I couldn't remember the last time I hugged my sister and felt this feeling of happiness. There was a time, growing up when I didn't like her. She would steal my clothes and wear them to school. She would take my favorite pillow and sleep with it at night. We had a strange sisterly love and hate for each other, but as time went on, we got closer.

My mom picked up Donavin, and he patted me on my back, further insinuating that everything was going to be okay. A few moments later, I felt my mom's warm nurturing hand in the middle of my back. This is what I'd missed while deployed—being surrounded by family, the family I didn't know I was going to need so desperately. My mother, sister, nephew, and I. Our little family, at that moment, were reunited.

2230 hours
"How old is this?" asked my sister as she headed toward the pullout bed in the corner of my room. With her back toward me, she held up a half-eaten chicken salad sandwich and smelled it.

"Is this old?" she nibbled a small bite.

"I've had that since lunchtime. It's probably no good by now," I said and laughter rang in my voice.

"Yuck," and she spat out the rock-hard bread.

"They have this little place downstairs that we can go to," I suggested. "They have smoothies, shakes, nachos, hamburgers, hot dogs … stuff like that."

She grabbed the couch cushions, her pillow, and the thin blanket, and placed them at the end of my bed.

"How big is this pull-out bed?" she asked, as she pushed the lever to extend the bed. "It's big. I mean, you will fit. You can sleep in my bed if that bed isn't good enough for you." I grabbed for my pillow.

"You can have my pillow too. It's bigger than yours." We both laughed. "I'm not sleeping in your bed, Brandi."

2300 hours

Drinking strawberry smoothies, eating nachos and hot dogs, my sister and I laughed all night. We didn't talk about cancer or how I felt about it. We never even mentioned the word "cancer."

Instead, we talked about shared memories from our childhood together—the time the TV fell on her when she was a kid and how we used to play on the Ouija board, asking to talk to Jesus Christ. We laughed about the times we played on the same soccer team—how one of our teammates stole her mood ring and I had to steal it back for her. Thinking about our childhood made me feel good and hopeful.

We ended our night with a fun and memorable photo shoot. We took a million pictures of us being silly with food in our mouths.

"Okay, it's your turn, Michelle," I said. "Put the bread in your mouth and say cheese."

Michelle crammed the whole hot dog in her mouth and laughed. Her plump lips spread wide and flat as mustard and ketchup oozed out from the sides of her mouth. Opened like a trap, her cheeks bulged and she said "Cheese." Looking at her that moment, I felt almost normal again. I felt like I was almost back to the real Brandi.

Flash. I took the picture.

EPILOGUE

It's been nine years since I discovered that strange lump that would drastically change my life. Before that day, I was a different person—very self-centered, taking life for granted and unaware that each breath I took was a gift. I was the type of person who could leave it all behind because I thought I knew best.

But now I know that everything in our life is susceptible to change. It's possible to go to bed and wake up to a new life. It's possible to have perfect health one day and the next day be presented with a change that you could have never fathomed.

I can no longer have children because of the harsh poisons I had in my body. I find it ironic that I saved my life, but I can no longer produce one. I also had my entire inner thigh muscle removed, which means that I can no longer sprint or run. It may sound odd, but this was probably the worst thing for me. I grew up very active and being told I couldn't run anymore or play any physical sports crushed me. I never wanted children. I didn't grow up planning my wedding day or imagining what my future husband would look like. Instead, I dreamt of playing soccer in the Olympics or for the Army. My dreams and aspirations came to a halt the day I was told that this cancer would take that away from me. A part of me died. In another part, Brandi was born. I am a stronger person. I love every moment, good and bad, big and small. Cancer shook me to the soul but granted me a second chance at being the person that I should have been all along. I now live my life as if every day is an adventure. I am more aware of everything around me, including my thoughts and the things I say to others and myself.

For some, living may mean getting up early, going to work, eating lunch on a break, coming home after work, and going to bed. I used to think that this was a life before cancer, that this was what "living" meant. Now I wake up feeling grateful and thankful for the day ahead of me and whatever I have planned for myself. I wake up and brush my teeth and list all the things that I am thankful for in my head. I wake up with a sense of purpose now instead of just going through the motions of life. Because of cancer,

I have truly been able to live a more fulfilling life.

I remember lying down in the hospital bed and promising myself to make my life more meaningful if I got to live and to write a book about my experience. I remember saying that our health is the most important thing that we have and that we all take good health for granted. Before cancer, I definitely didn't watch what I ate, and I didn't surround myself with positive, goal-oriented people. I do now. I know that in order to live a healthy life, you need good people around you, good health, and positive thoughts.

Being a cancer survivor is something that I am proud of, but I do find myself still wondering why. Why did I live? Why didn't my grandfather or the people I met at Walter Reed live? I am sure one day I will have the answers to these questions, but for now, I do not. All I know is that I have a second chance at life and I will make the best of it, and my mother was right, everything would be okay.

ABOUT THE AUTHOR

Brandi Benson is an American Writer, Speaker, Business Owner, and Cancer Survivor. She is also the founder and CEO of **Resume-Advantage**, an employment service for both civilians and transitioning military veterans. Her debut memoir tells the touching story of her Ewing Sarcoma diagnosis during her deployment in Iraq in 2008. With a BA in Mass Communications and Journalism at Ashford University and a Master of Fine Arts in Writing at the Savannah College of Art and Design. She is currently pursuing a Ph.D. in Education at Concordia University in Chicago. Brandi is dedicated to using her second chance at life to help fellow cancer survivors, participating weekly for the Livestrong cancer survivor program.

Connect with her on her official website -> www.BrandiLBenson.com

Made in the USA
Columbia, SC
17 July 2021

41889401R00064